CHECKERBOARD BIOGRAPHY LIBRARY

EXPLORERS

Daniel Boone

Kristin Petrie

ABDO
Publishing Company

visit us at
www.abdopub.com

Published by ABDO Publishing Company, 4940 Viking Drive, Edina, Minnesota 55435.
Copyright © 2004 by Abdo Consulting Group, Inc. International copyrights reserved in all
countries. No part of this book may be reproduced in any form without written permission from
the publisher.

Printed in the United States.

Cover Photos: Corbis, North Wind
Interior Photos: Corbis pp. 5, 6, 7, 9, 11, 15, 19, 21, 28, 29; Library of Congress p. 27; North Wind
    pp. 13, 23, 25

Series Coordinator: Stephanie Hedlund
Editors: Kate A. Conley, Kristin Van Cleaf
Art Direction & Cover Design: Neil Klinepier
Interior Design & Maps: Dave Bullen

Library of Congress Cataloging-in-Publication Data

Petrie, Kristin, 1970-
    Daniel Boone / Kristin Petrie.
       p. cm. -- (Explorers)
    Includes index.
    Summary: Describes the life and times of Daniel Boone, a man associated with the exploration
of Kentucky and the westward expansion of the American frontier.
    ISBN 1-59197-592-1
    1. Boone, Daniel, 1734-1820--Juvenile literature. 2. Pioneers--Kentucky--Biography--Juvenile
literature. 3. Explorers--Kentucky--Biography--Juvenile literature. 4. Frontier and pioneer life--
Kentucky--Juvenile literature. 5. Kentucky--Biography--Juvenile literature. 6. Kentucky--
Discovery and exploration--Juvenile literature. [1. Boone, Daniel, 1734-1820. 2. Pioneers. 3.
Explorers. 4. Frontier and pioneer life--Kentucky. 5. Kentucky--Discovery and exploration.] I.
Title.

F454.B66P48 2004
976.9'02'092--dc22
[B]   2003062921

Contents

Daniel Boone

Daniel Boone loved to explore. In the 1700s, people in the American colonies wondered what lay around the next corner. Most of the land was thick fields and dense forests. The wild frontier, as it was known, was any land west of the Appalachian Mountains.

During Boone's time, exploring the wilderness was **dangerous**. Native Americans felt threatened by European settlers. They sought to protect their food supply and way of life. Terrible fighting went on between the colonists and Native Americans throughout the next century.

There were also other risks in the frontier. Much of the country was untamed. There were wild animals and mountains. With all these dangers, why would anyone leave the safety of his or her home?

Daniel Boone was one of the brave men who continued to explore despite the dangers. He helped open the way to

	1451 Christopher Columbus born		1485 Hernán Cortés born	
1450 John Cabot born		1460 Vasco da Gama born		1491 Jacques Cartier born

the rest of the country. Continue reading to find out about Daniel Boone's many adventures.

Daniel Boone

1492
Columbus's first voyage west for Spain

1496
Cabot's first voyage for England

1493
Columbus's second voyage, attempted to colonize Hispaniola

Daniel's Family

In the 1600s, people from England came to America for many reasons. Some, such as the **Quakers**, were being **persecuted** for their religious beliefs. Others dreamed of owning land, which only the wealthy could do in England. To help these people, a Quaker named William Penn established the Pennsylvania Colony in 1682.

William Penn

Squire Boone, Daniel's father, was also a Quaker. Squire left England around 1712. He settled on the frontier of Pennsylvania with his brother and sister. The rest of their family joined them later.

In 1720, Squire married a Quaker woman named Sarah Morgan. Squire and Sarah were hardworking. The couple ran a farm, a weaving business, and a blacksmith's shop.

1497
Cabot's second voyage, discovered the Grand Banks; da Gama was first to sail around Africa to India

1496 or 1497
Hernando de Soto born

1498
Cabot's third voyage, may have died; Columbus's third voyage

Daniel Boone was born on November 2, 1734. He was the sixth of Sarah and Squire's 11 children. The family lived in a log cabin near the present-day city of Reading, Pennsylvania.

This house is located at the birthplace of Daniel Boone.

Would You?

Would you have been brave enough to journey across the ocean to the frontier? Do you think Squire Boone was brave?

1502
Columbus's fourth voyage; da Gama's second voyage

1506
Columbus died

1504
Cortés sailed to the West Indies

Young Woodsman

Daniel never had any formal education. But, he did learn to read, write, and use numbers. The restless youngster, however, was more interested in the outdoors.

Daniel's informal teachers were members of friendly Native American tribes. So, Daniel's schooling included hunting methods and woodcraft. He also learned Native American traditions, such as warfare **strategies**.

By the time he was 12 years old, Daniel was an exceptional hunter and woodsman. His family expected him to keep meat on the table!

In 1750, the Boones decided to move. They wanted to get away from other settlers and their **Quaker** roots. They left their farm and headed for North Carolina.

The new Boone home was near the Yadkin River, on the edge of the wilderness. Can you imagine how happy this made young Daniel Boone?

1511
Cortés helped take over Cuba

1510
Francisco Vásquez de Coronado born

1514
De Soto went to the New World

This excitement came with a price, however. The Cherokee and Shawnee of this region were especially **dangerous**. To protect their hunting grounds, these tribes would attack without warning. The Boone family was always in danger.

This 1700s drawing shows a woodsman hunting game.

Before Exploring

In 1754, the French and Indian War began. In this war, the French and English fought over the Ohio Valley region. The French government had built Fort Duquesne on the Ohio River. British **major general** Edward Braddock had come to America to reclaim this **strategic** site.

Braddock was used to open fields for battle. But, the French and their Native American **allies** used a different type of warfare. They **ambushed** the British soldiers from hiding places in the thick forests.

Daniel drove supply wagons for the British in this war. On July 9, 1755, he was involved in an ambush. When the British retreated, he cut his horses free from the wagons and escaped. The British troops were defeated before they could reach Fort Duquesne.

1524
Da Gama's third voyage, died in Cochin, India

1519–1521
Cortés conquered the Aztec Empire and claimed Mexico for Spain

1532
De Soto helped attack the Inca Empire

Daniel returned home to North Carolina. There, he became interested in a young woman. Her name was Rebecca Bryan.

Major General Braddock and his troops being ambushed during the French and Indian War

Twenty-one-year-old Daniel showed Rebecca and her parents his abilities as a hunter and woodsman. He showed them he could feed his family well and provide a good income. Rebecca and Daniel were married in 1756.

The Boones soon moved to a small farm on the Bryan settlement. For the next ten years, they stayed in North Carolina. They farmed, and Daniel earned extra money as a wagoner. Each fall and winter, however, the outdoorsman went on long hunting trips.

In the late 1750s, Daniel and Rebecca started their family. During her husband's absences, Rebecca raised and cared for their children. She grew their vegetables and cooked wild **game**. This courageous woman also protected her family from many hostile **intruders**.

During the late 1700s, frontier settlements were open to attacks by Native American tribes. Bandits were also a danger. A number of times, the Boones took shelter in nearby military forts for protection against these attacks.

1534
Cartier's first voyage for France

1539–1542
De Soto explored La Florida

1533
De Soto helped take over Cuzco

1535
Cartier's second voyage

Would You?

Would you want to be left alone on the frontier? Why do you think Rebecca Boone stayed in the wilderness with her children?

Exploring Florida

In 1763, the English government received Florida from Spain in a treaty. The English offered the settlers in the northern colonies free land, just for going there! This was an offer Daniel Boone could not refuse.

In late summer 1765, Boone and a small group began their journey. The men cut their way through hundreds of miles of southern wilderness. When they arrived in Florida, they found that the land was filled with swamps, snakes, and bugs. But, Boone still claimed a piece of land there.

Boone raced back home in time for Christmas dinner. He was excited to share his experience with his family. However, his wife refused to move to Florida. Boone was forced to think of a new adventure.

For many years, Boone had wanted to see what lay on the other side of the Appalachian Mountains. He had been told about a land called Kentucky. But, conflicts with Native

1541
Cartier's third voyage, attempted to colonize Canada; Cortés volunteered to fight against Algiers

1540
Coronado set out to find the Seven Cities of Cíbola; Francis Drake born

Americans had led the English government to discourage further settlement there.

Boone followed his dream anyway. He left to explore the region in 1767. On this trip, Boone and a companion hunted and trapped. They hoped to get rich from selling furs. The men were later caught in a sudden snowstorm. They spent the winter in Kentucky, and returned home in 1768.

Boone encountered vast areas of swamp in Florida. This type of wetland was difficult for growing crops.

1547
Cortés died

1557
Cartier died

1542
Coronado returned to New Spain; de Soto died

1554
Coronado died

1566
Drake's first voyage to the New World

The Journeys of Daniel Boone

1765 ⟶ ———————	
1769 AND 1775 ⟶ ———————	
1799 ⟶ ———————	

Nebraska

Missouri River

Kansas

Arizona

New Mexico

Oklahoma

Texas

N

MEXICO

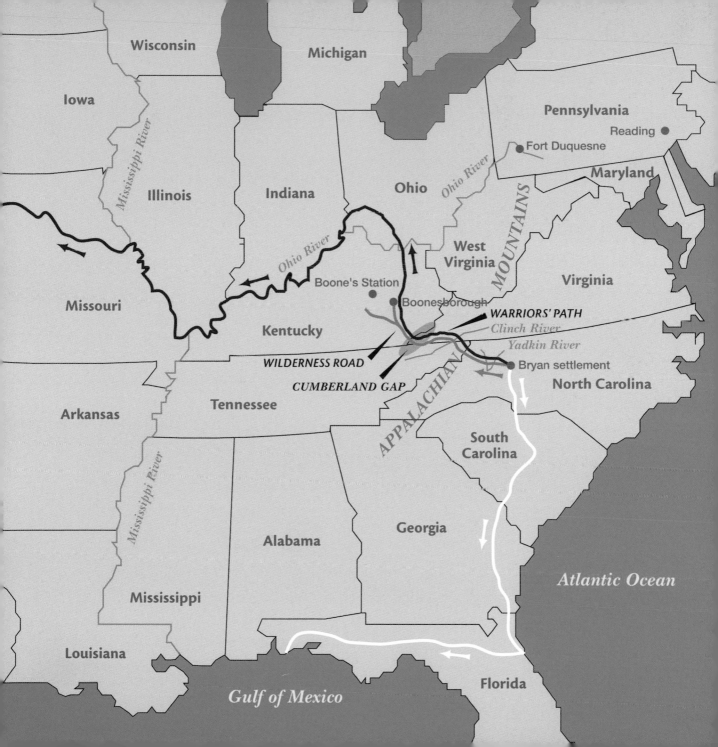

Cumberland Gap

In 1768, an old friend visited Boone's home. Frontiersman John Finley wanted to find an easy way into Kentucky from North Carolina and Virginia. Until then, getting across the mountain range was difficult and **dangerous**. But, he had heard there was a gap through the Cumberland Mountains.

Finley asked Boone to lead the expedition. Boone accepted the challenge. A team of explorers left North Carolina in the spring of 1769.

The team eventually came across the Warriors' Path. It was used by Native Americans on their way to war with other tribes. The team followed the path, and it took them to the break in the mountain range. It was named the Cumberland Gap.

What the group found on the other side was exactly what they'd hoped for. The land was made of rich soil that was perfect for farming. Huge herds of buffalo roamed the

1567
Drake's second voyage

1577
Drake began a worldwide voyage, was first Englishman to sail the Pacific Ocean

1570 and 1572
Drake terrorized the Spanish in the New World

prairies. Deer, turkeys, and other **game** filled the forests. It was a woodsman's paradise.

Not surprisingly, Boone stayed for two years. After a number of adventures, Boone went home. But, he soon returned to Kentucky and settled there.

The Cumberland Gap

Wilderness Road

In 1773, Boone's family and a group of neighbors headed west. Native American tribes were angry that settlers were intruding on their hunting grounds. So, a group of them captured and killed Boone's oldest son and another boy. After the attack, the pioneers abandoned their mission.

This tragedy sparked anger among pioneers along the entire frontier. Soon, terrible acts were taking place against Native American tribes. In **retaliation**, the Cherokee and other tribes joined forces with the Shawnee.

The Boone family settled near the Clinch River in Virginia. Boone joined the Virginia **militia**, and the fighting began. Eventually, the militia overtook the Native American warriors in a major battle. It took place in what is now the state of West Virginia.

After the fighting, Boone blazed the trail known as the Wilderness Road. It was his most notable accomplishment.

1588
Drake helped England win the Battle of Gravelines against Spain's Invincible Armada

1581
Drake knighted by Queen Elizabeth I

1596
Drake died

The Wilderness Road

1728
James Cook born

1765
Boone journeyed to Florida

1768
Cook sailed for Tahiti

1734
Daniel Boone born

1767
Boone explored Kentucky

He performed this task in 1775, after Judge Richard Henderson formed the Transylvania Company.

The Transylvania Company purchased a **tract** of land in Kentucky from the Cherokee. Henderson wanted a faster way for settlers to get to and colonize the region. So, he asked Daniel Boone, by now a notable explorer, to help him.

Boone and a team of experienced woodsmen truly did blaze a trail. It began as a connection of warpaths and buffalo **traces**. The woods were so thick it seemed no person had been there before.

Think of a dirt-bike path that needs to be made wide enough for a minivan. The woodsmen did something similar, but without bulldozers!

Starting in Virginia, the Wilderness Road went west through the Appalachian Mountains. Once through the Cumberland Gap, the trail continued northwestward into Kentucky. The Wilderness Road opened the door to the rest of the nation!

Boone points toward Kentucky.

1778
Cook became the first European to record Hawaiian Islands; Boone captured by Shawnee

1775
Boone cut the Wilderness Road from Virginia to Kentucky

1779
Cook died

Boonesborough

Near the end of the Wilderness Road, the settlers founded a colony. They named it Boonesborough, after Daniel Boone. Soon, Judge Henderson arrived with more settlers for the new colony.

At about the same time, Boone moved his wife and children to the Kentucky frontier. Soon, more conflicts arose between the settlers and Native Americans. Many settlers found Kentucky too **dangerous**. They fled the new territory shortly after arriving.

The year 1778 was difficult for Daniel Boone. He was captured while on an expedition to find salt. But, rather than kill the famous frontiersman, the Shawnee decided to bring Boone into their tribe. Boone pretended to adopt their ways.

However, when Boone heard the Shawnee planned to attack Boonesborough, he escaped. Boone raced back to

1813
John C. Frémont born

1842
Frémont's first independent surveying mission

1820
Boone died

the settlement. He prepared the settlement and the pioneers for the coming siege.

Soon, 400 Shawnee surrounded the fort and demanded surrender. About 50 men, with their wives and children inside, fought back. The Shawnee's attack failed, and the tribe soon retreated.

The Shawnee attacked Boonesborough in two ways. They set the fort's roof and walls on fire. They also dug a tunnel to get under the fort.

Would You?

Would you know how to defend a fort against 400 attackers? How do you think Boone prepared for this?

Boone's Station

Many settlers wondered if Boone had helped the Shawnee attack Boonesborough. They wondered whether he'd surrendered the settlers to the Shawnee. Boone was tried by a military court, but found innocent.

For his part in saving Boonesborough, Boone was promoted to **major** in the **militia**. Boone soon left Boonesborough to rejoin his family. When he had been captured, Rebecca had moved their children back to North Carolina. She thought her husband had died in **captivity**.

Eventually, the Boone family returned to Kentucky and founded a new settlement. Boone's Station is now called Booneville, Kentucky.

In 1780, Boone was promoted to **lieutenant colonel**. He helped defend the settlement against native raids. In 1784, writer John Filson documented Boone's many adventures and accomplishments. Daniel Boone became famous.

1856
Frémont ran for president of the United States but lost

1845-1846
Frémont explored the Great Basin and the Pacific Coast, fought in the Mexican War

1890
Frémont died

In 1792, Kentucky became the fifteenth state in the Union. The government refused to recognize some of Boone's land claims in Kentucky. So, Boone headed for Missouri in 1799.

This document from the House of Representatives discusses the refusal of Boone's land claim in Kentucky.

11th CONGRESS.

No. 161.

2d SESSION.

GRANT TO DANIEL BOONE.

COMMUNICATED TO THE SENATE JANUARY 12, 1810.

Mr. MEIGS, from the committee to whom was referred the petition of Daniel Boone, together with the bill for his relief, made the following report:

That, at a period antecedent to the revolutionary war, Daniel Boone, the petitioner, possessing an ardent desire for the exploration of the (then) Western wilderness of the United States, after traversing a length of mountainous and uninhabited country, discovered and, with a few bold and enterprising fellows, established, with a perilous hardihood, the first settlement of civilized population in the (now) State of Kentucky. That, in maintaining the possession of that country, until the peace of 1783, he experienced all the vicissitudes of a war with enemies the most daring, insidious, and cruel, and which were aided by Canadians from the British provinces of Upper Canada; and that during that long contest he lost several children by the hands of the savages.

That it appears to the committee, that although the petitioner was not *officially employed* by the Government of the United States, yet that he was *actually engaged* against their enemies, through the whole of the war of the Revolution.

That in the exploring, settling, and defending that country, he eminently contributed to the early march of the American Western population, and which has redounded to the benefit of the United States. That your petitioner is old, infirm, and, though dependent on agriculture, by adverse and unpropitious circumstances, possesses not one acre of that immeasurable territory which he so well defended, after having been the pioneer of its settlement. The petitioner disclaiming all idea of a demand upon the justice of his country, yet requests, as a grateful benevolence, that Congress would grant him some reasonable portion of land in the territory of Louisiana. The committee, upon the whole circumstances of the merit and situation of the petitioner, beg leave to report the bill without amendment.

To the Senate and Representatives of the citizens of the United States in Congress assembled. The petition of Daniel Boone, at present an inhabitant of the territory of Louisiana, respectfully showeth:

That your petitioner has spent a long life in exploring the wilds of North America; and has, by his own personal exertions, been greatly instrumental in opening the road to civilization in the immense territories now attached to the United States, and, in some instances, matured into independent States.

An ardent thirst for discovery, united with a desire to benefit a rising family, has impelled him to encounter the numerous hardships, privations, difficulties, and dangers to which he has unavoidably been exposed. How far his desire for discovery has been extended, and what consequences have resulted from his labors, are, at this time, unnecessary to detail.

But, while your petitioner has thus opened the way to thousands, to countries possessed of every natural advantage, and although he may have gratified to excess his thirst for discovery, he has to lament that he has not derived those personal advantages which his exertions would seem to have merited. He has secured but a scanty portion of that immeasurable territory over which his discoveries have extended, and his family have reason to regret that their interest had not been more the great object of his discoveries.

Your petitioner has nothing to demand from the justice of his country, but he respectfully suggests, that it might be deemed an act of grateful benevolence, if his country, amidst their bounties, would so far gratify his wish, as to grant him some reasonable portion of land within the territory of Louisiana.

He is the more induced to this request, as the favorite pittance of soil to which he conceived he had acquired a title, under the Spanish Government, has been wrested from him by a construction of the existing laws not in his contemplation, and beyond his foresight. Your petitioner is not disposed to murmur or complain; but conscious of the value and extent of his services, he solicits some evidence of their liberality.

He approaches the august assemblage of his fellow-citizens with a confidence inspired by that spirit which has led him so often to the deep recesses of the wilds of America; and he flatters himself that he with his family will be induced to acknowledge that the United States knows how to appreciate and encourage the efforts of her citizens, in enterprises of magnitude, from which proportionate public good may be derived.

DANIEL BOONE.

1910
Jacques Cousteau born

1951
Cousteau's first expedition in the Red Sea

1942
Cousteau and Gagnan developed the Aqua-Lung for diving

Boone's Legacy

In Missouri, the Spanish lieutenant governor promised Boone a huge amount of land. He hoped Boone's name would attract other settlers to the colony.

Daniel Boone

In 1800, Missouri was part of an area called the Louisiana Territory. In that year, Spain sold the territory to France. France then sold the Louisiana Territory to the United States.

After the final sale, Boone lost much of the land he had claimed in Missouri. The U.S. government refused to acknowledge his land grants there, too. However, it later granted Boone 850 acres (344 ha) for his services. But he was forced to sell it to pay debts.

In 1813, Rebecca died at the age of 73. Boone's health was also failing. He hunted close to home due to **arthritis**. In

1820, just before turning 86, the national hero died. His family buried him in Kentucky, next to his wife.

Daniel Boone spent his life exploring. A natural leader, Boone cleared the way across the mountains and guided settlers to the West. He established settlements, served in war, and fought for the right to live freely.

Daniel Boone's gravestone stands in Frankfort, Kentucky.

Would You?

Would you want to move as often as Daniel Boone did? Why do you think Boone loved to explore?

Glossary

allies - people or countries that agree to help each other in times of need.

ambush - a surprise attack from a hidden position.

arthritis - a medical condition of inflamed joints that causes much pain.

captivity - the state of being captured and held against one's will.

dangerous - able or likely to cause injury or harm.

game - wild animals hunted for food or sport.

intruder - a person who enters an area, such as another person's home, without permission.

lieutenant colonel - a military rank above a major and below a colonel.

major - a military rank above a captain and below a lieutenant colonel.

major general - a military rank above brigadier general and below lieutenant general.

militia - a group of citizens trained for war or emergencies.

persecute - to harass someone because of his or her origin, religion, or other beliefs.

Quaker - a member of the religious group called the Society of Friends.

retaliation - the act of paying back a wrong or injury.

strategy - a plan for battle.

trace - a path, trail, or road made by a person or animal that has passed through an area.

tract - an area of land.

Saying It

Appalachian - ah-puh-LAY-chuhn
arthritis - ahr-THREYE-tuhs
Boonesborough - BOONZ-buhr-oh
Fort Duquesne - FOHRT duh-KAYN
militia - muh-LIH-shuh
Transylvania - tran-suhl-VAY-nyuh

Web Sites

To learn more about Daniel Boone, visit ABDO Publishing
Company on the World Wide Web at **www.abdopub.com**.
Web sites about Daniel Boone are featured on our Book
Links page. These links are routinely monitored and
updated to provide the most current information available.

Jacques Cousteau   *Sir Francis Drake*   *Vasco da Gama*

Hernán Cortés   *Hernando de Soto*   *John C. Frémont*

Index